Bible Study Series
for senior high

Loveland, Colorado

Why Creation Matters
Core Belief Bible Study Series

Credits
Editors: Lisa Baba Lauffer and Karl Leuthauser
Creative Development Editor: Michael D. Warden
Chief Creative Officer: Joani Schultz
Copy Editor: Dena Twinem
Art Director: Bill Fisher
Computer Graphic Artist: Ray Tollison
Photographer: Craig DeMartino
Production Manager: Gingar Kunkel

Unless otherwise noted, Scriptures quoted from The Youth Bible, New Century Version, copyright © 1991 by Word Publishing, Dallas, Texas 75039. Used by permission.

ISBN 0-7644-0880-1
10 9 8 7 6 5 4 3 2 1   06 05 04 03 02 01 00 99 98 97

Printed in the United States of America.

Bible Study Series
for senior high

contents:

the Core Belief: ▼Creation

Debates rage about how the world came into existence. Did God create it in seven twenty-four-hour days? Did some kind of cosmic meeting of atoms explode into what we now call the universe? Your young people are in the middle of these debates, and they need answers.

God created everything that exists. Having no existing materials to work with, God created the universe by speaking it into existence, then forming this matter into an incredible variety of entities. His creation of the world was purposeful and has value. While everything God created was originally good, humanity sinned and brought suffering and death into God's creation. But God continues to guide his creation, and in the end, when he's completed his plan for evil and Satan, he'll create a new earth and a new heaven where there will be no more crying, pain, or death.

the ▼Helpful Stuff

the ▼ Studies

▼Creation as a Core Christian Belief

The Bible begins with a simple declaration: "In the beginning God created the sky and the earth" (Genesis 1:1). That simple truth forms the foundation for all of Christian thought—about the world around us, the nature of humanity, even eternal life itself.

For example, the Bible teaches that every part of God's creation is good. Consequently, everything that God created has value. Therefore, we shouldn't degrade, debase, or treat with contempt anything God has made, including ourselves and the world around us. Also, when God created us, he gave us responsibility and a purpose for living: God placed us on this earth to represent him and to take care of his creation.

In the first study of *Why Creation Matters,* kids will deal with one of the greatest challenges to the Christian faith: **evolution.** Kids will be given tools to evaluate the truth of God's creation and his existence. They'll deal with some of the tough issues surrounding their own existence and will have an opportunity to see that it makes rational sense that God created the universe.

In the second study, your kids will look at the effect that sin has had on God's good and perfect creation. They'll have an opportunity to discover that God didn't intend for his creation to be subject to pain, sorrow, and **discouragement.** God's creation has been poisoned by sin, and we all must face the consequences of our fallen state.

In the third study, students will examine the **mysteries of the world** that surround their daily lives. As they contemplate the complexity of the human immune system or the limitlessness of space, they'll have no choice but to see the work of a majestic and powerful Creator. They'll be encouraged to notice the reflection of God's beauty and to realize that his creation surpasses our imagination.

In the final study of this book, kids will be challenged to react to the beauty and majesty of the Creator by caring for his creation. As they talk and learn about **the environment,** kids will be encouraged to live out their faith in God by "ruling over" creation with responsibility and care.

It's easy for young people today to lose sight of the important issues relating to creation. Too often they're distracted by the "battle" between Creation and evolution or the various disagreements between Christians who interpret the biblical Creation story differently. However, if your kids focus on the clear biblical teachings on creation, they can go into the world with a clear sense of who they are and where they fit within God's creation.

For a more comprehensive look at this Core Christian Belief, read Group's **Get Real: Making Core Christian Beliefs Relevant to Teenagers.**

DEPTHFINDER

HOW THE BIBLE DESCRIBES CREATION

To help you effectively guide your kids toward this Core Christian Belief, use these overviews as a launching point for a more in-depth study of Creation:

● **God created all things that exist.** God, whose name means "I Am," is the only self-existing being. Everything else in the spiritual and physical worlds was created by God (Genesis 1:1; Isaiah 45:12; John 1:3; Ephesians 3:9b; and Revelation 4:11).

● **God's first creative act brought the materials of the universe into existence.** God is eternal, but matter is not. God didn't use pre-existing materials to make the heavens and the earth. Rather, God created all that exists out of nothing simply by calling it into existence (Genesis 1:1; Mark 13:19; Romans 4:17; and Hebrews 11:3).

● **In later creative acts, God shaped matter into different entities.** After God called matter into existence, he shaped it into different objects and forms of life. For example, he created humans and animals out of the "dust of the ground" (Genesis 1:9-25; 2:4b-22; Job 33:6; Psalm 103:13-14; and 2 Peter 3:5).

● **God continues to preserve and guide the creation.** God didn't set the world in motion and leave it to run on its own. God holds the universe together, maintains its existence, and guides it to accomplish his purposes (Nehemiah 9:6; Daniel 4:34-35; Matthew 6:26-30; 10:29; Colossians 1:17; and Hebrews 1:3).

● **Everything that God created was originally good.** God designed and created the world so that everything in it lived in complete harmony and perfect fulfillment of the purpose for which God had created it. However, human sin polluted God's good creation and introduced death, disharmony, and destruction (Genesis 1:4, 10, 12, 18, 25, 31; 3:1-19; Proverbs 3:19-20; and 1 Timothy 4:4).

● **God created everything for a reason.** Nothing in God's creation is a product of chance. Everything has a purpose. For example, the planets and stars declare God's magnificence. As humans, we represent God on earth (Genesis 1:26-28; 2:18-24; 1 Chronicles 16:30-33; Psalms 8:3-8; 19:1-4a; and Revelation 4:11).

● **Everything that God created has value.** Since God created everything for some specific purpose, everything has value. Consequently, we shouldn't treat any part of the creation with contempt. Rather, we should treat everything with respect as God does (Job 38; Jonah 4:10-11; and Matthew 5:43-45; 6:26-30).

● **In the future, God will create a new heaven and earth.** Human sin corrupted God's creation, but God will accomplish his plan for creation. After God defeats Satan and sin and death, he will re-establish his creation in its original goodness and perfection (Isaiah 65:17-19; Romans 8:18-21; 1 Corinthians 15:20-28; Colossians 1:19-20; and Revelation 21:1–22:5).

CORE CHRISTIAN BELIEF OVERVIEW

Here are the twenty-four Core Christian Belief categories that form the backbone of Core Belief Bible Study Series:

The Nature of God	Jesus Christ	The Holy Spirit
Humanity	Evil	Suffering
Creation	The Spiritual Realm	The Bible
Salvation	Spiritual Growth	Personal Character
God's Justice	Sin & Forgiveness	The Last Days
Love	The Church	Worship
Authority	Prayer	Family
Service	Relationships	Sharing Faith

Look for Group's Core Belief Bible Study Series books in these other Core Christian Beliefs!

about

core belief

Bible Study Series
for senior high

Think for a moment about your young people. When your students walk out of your youth program after they graduate from junior high or high school, what do you want them to know? What foundation do you want them to have so they can make wise choices?

You probably want them to know the essentials of the Christian faith. You want them to base everything they do on the foundational truths of Christianity. Are you meeting this goal?

If you have any doubt that your kids will walk into adulthood knowing and living by the tenets of the Christian faith, then you've picked up the right book. All the books in Group's Core Belief Bible Study Series encourage young people to discover the essentials of Christianity and to put those essentials into practice. Let us explain...

What Is Group's Core Belief Bible Study Series?

Group's Core Belief Bible Study Series is a biblically in-depth study series for junior high and senior high teenagers. This Bible study series utilizes four defining commitments to create each study. These "plumb lines" provide structure and continuity for every activity, study, project, and discussion. They are:

● **A Commitment to Biblical Depth**—Core Belief Bible Study Series is founded on the belief that kids not only *can* understand the deeper truths of the Bible but also *want* to understand them. Therefore, the activities and studies in this series strive to explain the "why" behind every truth we explore. That way, kids learn principles, not just rules.

● **A Commitment to Relevance**—Most kids aren't interested in abstract theories or doctrines about the universe. They want to know how to live successfully right now, today, in the heat of problems they can't ignore. Because of this, each study connects a real-life need with biblical principles that speak directly to that need. This study series finally bridges the gap between Bible truths and the real-world issues kids face.

● **A Commitment to Variety**—Today's young people have been raised in a sound bite world. They demand variety. For that reason, no two meetings in this study series are shaped exactly the same.

● **A Commitment to Active and Interactive Learning**—Active learning is learning by doing. Interactive learning simply takes active learning a step further by having kids teach each other what they've learned. It's a process that helps kids internalize and remember their discoveries.

For a more detailed description of these concepts, see the section titled "Why Active and Interactive Learning Works With Teenagers" beginning on page 57.

So how can you accomplish all this in a set of four easy-to-lead Bible studies? By weaving together various "power" elements to produce a fun experience that leaves kids challenged and encouraged.

Turn the page to take a look at some of the power elements used in this series.

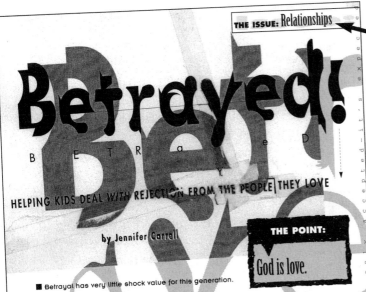

THE ISSUE: Relationships

Betrayed!

HELPING KIDS DEAL WITH REJECTION FROM THE PEOPLE THEY LOVE

by Jennifer Carrell

THE POINT:

God is love.

■ Betrayal has very little shock value for this generation. It's as commonplace as compact discs and mosh pits. For many kids today, betrayal characterizes their parents' wedding vows. It's part of their curriculum at school; it defines the headlines and evening news. Betrayal is not only accepted—it's expected. ■ At the heart of such acceptance lies the belief that nothing is absolute. No vow, no law, no promise can be trusted. Relationships are betrayed at the earliest convenience. Repeatedly, kids see that something called "love" lasts just as long as it's [convenient] permanence. But deep inside, they hunger to see a

The Study AT A GLANCE

SECTION	MINUTES	WHAT STUDENTS WILL DO	SUPPLIES
Discussion Starter	up to 5	JUMP-START—Identify some of the most common themes in today's movies.	Newsprint, marker
Investigation of Betrayal	12 to 15	REALITY CHECK—Form groups to compare anonymous, real-life stories of betrayal with experiences in their own lives.	"Profiles of Betrayal" handouts (p. 20), highlighter pens, newsprint, marker, tape
	3 to 5	WHO BETRAYED WHOM?—Guess the identities of the people profiled in the handouts.	Paper, tape, pen
Investigation of True Love	15 to 18	SOURCE WORK—Study and discuss God's definition of perfect love.	Bibles, newsprint, marker
	5 to 7	LOVE MESSAGES—Create unique ways to send a "message of love" to the victims of betrayal they've been studying.	Newsprint, markers, tape
Personal Application	10 to 15	SYMBOLIC LOVE—Give a partner a personal symbol of perfect love.	Paper lunch sack, pens, scissors, paper, catalogs

notes:

Betrayed! 16

● **A Relevant Topic**—More than ever before, kids live in the now. What matters to them and what attracts their hearts is what's happening in their world at this moment. For this reason, every Core Belief Bible Study focuses on a particular hot topic that kids care about.

● **A Core Christian Belief**—Group's Core Belief Bible Study Series organizes the wealth of Christian truth and experience into twenty-four Core Christian Belief categories. These twenty-four headings act as umbrellas for a collection of detailed beliefs that define Christianity and set it apart from the world and every other religion. Each book in this series features one Core Christian Belief with lessons suited for junior high or senior high students.

"But," you ask, "won't my kids be bored talking about all these spiritual beliefs?" No way! As a youth leader, you know the value of using hot topics to connect with young people. Ultimately teenagers talk about issues because they're searching for meaning in their lives. They want to find the one equation that will make sense of all the confusing events happening around them. Each Core Belief Bible Study answers that need by connecting a hot topic with a powerful Christian principle. Kids walk away from the study with something more solid than just the shifting ebb and flow of their own opinions. They walk away with a deeper understanding of their Christian faith.

● **The Point**—This simple statement is designed to be the intersection between the Core Christian Belief and the hot topic. Everything in the study ultimately focuses on The Point so that kids study it and allow it time to sink into their hearts.

● **The Study at a Glance**—A quick look at this chart will tell you what kids will do, how long it will take them to do it, and what supplies you'll need to get it done.

● **The Bible Connection**—This is the power base of each study. Whether it's just one verse or several chapters, The Bible Connection provides the vital link between kids' minds and their hearts. The content of each Core Belief Bible Study reflects the belief that the true power of God—the power to expose, heal, and change kids' lives—is contained in his Word.

God is love.

THE BIBLE CONNECTION

1 JOHN 4:7-21   The Apostle John explains the nature and definition of perfect love.

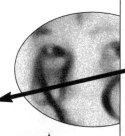

I n this study, kids will compare the imperfect love defined in real-life stories of betrayal to God's definition of perfect love.

By making this comparison, kids can discover that God is love and therefore incapable of betraying them. Then they'll be able to recognize the incredible opportunity God offers to experience the only relationship worthy of their absolute trust.

Explore the verses in The Bible Connect mation in the Depthfinder boxes throughou understanding of how these Scriptures con

THE STUDY

DISCUSSION STARTER ▼

Jump-Start (up to 5 minutes) As kids arrive, ask them to thi common themes in movies, books, TV sho have kids each contribute ideas for a mas two other kids in the room and sharing sider providing copies of People maga what's currently showing on televisio their suggestions, write their respons **come up with a lot of great ide** ent, look through this list an ments most of these theme

After kids make several s responses are connected

● **Why do you think**

Betrayed!   **17**

LEADER TIP for The Study

Because this topic can be so powerful and relevant to kids' lives, your group members may be tempted to get caught up in issues and lose sight of the deeper biblical principle found in The Point. Help your kids grasp The Point by guiding kids to focus on the biblical investigation and discussing how God's truth connects with reality in their lives.

DEPTHFINDER   UNDERSTANDING INTEGRITY

Your students may not be entirely familiar with the meaning of integrity, especially as it might apply to God's character in the Trinity. Use these definitions (taken from Webster's II New Riverside Dictionary) and other information to help you guide kids toward a better understanding of how God maintains integrity through the three expressions of the Trinity.

Integrity: 1. Firm adherence to a code or standard of values. 2. The state of being unimpaired. 3. The quality or condition of being undivided.

Synonyms for integrity include probity, completeness, wholeness, soundness, and perfection.

Our word "integrity" comes from the Latin word *integritas*, which means soundness. *Integritas* is also the root of the word "integer," which means "whole or complete," as in a "whole" number.

The Hebrew word that's often translated "integrity" (for example, in Psalm 25:21 [NIV]) is *tam*. It means whole, perfect, sincere, and honest.

CREATIVE GOD-EXPLORATION ▼

Top Hats (18 to 20 minutes) Form three groups, with each trio member from the previous activity going to a different group. Give each group Bibles, paper, and pens and assign each group a different hat God wears: Father, Son, or Holy Spirit.

● **Depthfinder Boxes**—These informative sidelights located throughout each study add insight into a particular passage, word, historical fact, or Christian doctrine. Depthfinder boxes also provide insight into teen culture, adolescent development, current events, and philosophy.

● **Leader Tips**—These handy information boxes coach you through the study, offering helpful suggestions on everything from altering activities for different-sized groups to streamlining discussions to using effective discipline techniques.

Holy Profiles

Your assigned Bible passage describes how a particular person or group responded when confronted with God's holiness. Use the information in your passage to help your group discuss the questions below. Then use your flashlights to teach the other two groups what you discover.

■ Based on your passage, what does holiness look like?

■ What does holiness sound like?

■ When people see God's holiness, how does it affect them?

■ How is this response to God's holiness like humility?

■ Based on your passage, how would you describe humility?

■ Why is humility an appropriate human response to God's holiness?

■ Based on what you see in your passage, do you think you are a humble person? Why or why not?

■ What's one way you could develop humility in your life this week?

● **Handouts**—Most Core Belief Bible Studies include photocopiable handouts to use with your group. Handouts might take the form of a fun game, a lively discussion starter, or a challenging study page for kids to take home—anything to make your study more meaningful and effective.

The Last Word on Core Belief Bible Studies

Soon after you begin to use Group's Core Belief Bible Study Series, you'll see signs of real growth in your group members. Your kids will gain a deeper understanding of the Bible and of their own Christian faith. They'll see more clearly how a relationship with Jesus affects their daily lives. And they'll grow closer to God.

But that's not all. You'll also see kids grow closer to one another.

That's because this series is founded on the principle that Christian faith grows best in the context of relationship. Each study uses a variety of interactive pairs and small groups and always includes discussion questions that promote deeper relationships. The friendships kids will build through this study series will enable them to grow *together* toward a deeper relationship with God.

creation and evolution

Creation & Evolution

RECONCILING FAITH AND SCIENCE

by Michael D. Warden

■ We live in an incredible universe.

■ Just look around. Creation is full of a host of wonders—from galaxies to gorillas, pulsars to pine trees, light-years to lightning bugs. It's simply marvelous, no doubt about it. But a few questions remain unanswered...

THE POINT:

God created the universe.

■ How did creation get here? Was a Creator involved, or was it merely the result of chance? *Where was God when the world began?* ■ Public schools tell your kids one answer to those questions. Churches tell them another. And young people are caught in the middle. But the question "Where was God when the world began?" only points kids toward a deeper, more relevant question in their lives: "Where is God today?" ■ This study takes a critical look at both creationism and evolution, examining the arguments that have kept scientists and theologians at odds for over one hundred years. And it leads kids to discover one simple truth—that no theory of the world's origins makes sense apart from the existence of God.

The Study
AT A GLANCE

SECTION	MINUTES	WHAT STUDENTS WILL DO	SUPPLIES
Theory Construction	15 to 20	THEORETICAL SPUD—Create towers that represent their theories of the universe's origins.	Potatoes, plastic utensils, markers, "Evolution—Yes!" handouts (p. 22), "Creationism—Yes!" handouts (p. 23)
	up to 5	SPUD TO SPUD—Use their towers to teach each other their theories.	Newsprint, markers, tape
Unity Prayer	up to 5	SPUD LINKS—Pray for each other to learn from God's Spirit during this study.	Potatoes, markers
Theory Collapse	15 to 20	FALLEN SPUDS—Use logical arguments to try to dismantle their opponents' tower.	"Evolution—No!" handouts (p. 24), "Creationism—No!" handouts (p. 24),
Debriefing	10 to 15	THIS SPUD'S FOR YOU—Debrief the experience and exchange potato blessings.	Bibles, fresh potatoes, markers

notes:

THE POINT OF *CREATION AND EVOLUTION:*

God created the universe.

THE BIBLE CONNECTION

GENESIS 1–2	God creates the universe.
JOB 38:1-33	God challenges Job to explain how the universe was created.

I n this study, kids will form groups and build towers that represent either the theory of evolution or creationism. Then they'll use logical arguments to try to collapse each other's theories.

Through this experience, kids can learn the strengths and weaknesses of both theories and discover how impossible it is to explain the origin of the universe apart from the existence of God.

Explore the verses in The Bible Connection, then examine the information in the Depthfinder box to gain a deeper understanding of how these Scriptures connect with your young people.

BEFORE THE STUDY

Before kids arrive, you'll need to purchase enough raw potatoes so each person can have two. You'll also need twenty potatoes for constructing "theories." Make sure the potatoes are fairly small. (If you would rather not use potatoes, you can use plastic-foam balls, marshmallows, or fruit.) You'll also need two or three packages of plastic knives or forks (avoid spoons, since they don't work as well for this project). Set the potatoes, along with the other supplies, in the center of the room.

Make one photocopy of each of the handouts for every two people you expect.

LEADER TIP for The Study

Because this topic can be so powerful and relevant to kids' lives, your group members may be tempted to get caught up in issues and lose sight of the deeper biblical principle found in The Point. Help your kids grasp The Point by guiding kids to focus on the biblical investigation and discussing how God's truth connects with reality in their lives.

LEADER TIP

for Theory Construction

Your students will be creating towers based upon two theories about the origin of the universe: evolution and creationism. The fundamental difference between these two theories is in their views about God's existence. Evolutionists approach scientific evidence with the assumption that a creator God doesn't exist. Creationists approach the same evidence with the assumption that a creator God does exist. Because of their differing assumptions, these two theories can often draw drastically different conclusions from the same body of evidence.
Point out this difference to kids as they work to build their theories. It will make it easier for them to tell the two theories apart.

THE STUDY

THEORY CONSTRUCTION ▼

Theoretical Spud (15 to 20 minutes)
Once everyone has arrived, form two groups: the Evolutionists and the Creationists. Distribute copies of the "Evolution—Yes!" handout (p. 22) to the Evolutionists and copies of the "Creationism—Yes!" handout (p. 23) to the Creationists. Say: **Your job is to work together with your group to build a tower that represents your assigned theory about the origin of the universe. Your handout provides you with research information and instructs you in how to build your theory.**

Point out the potatoes, markers, and plastic utensils you placed in the center of the room. Say: **You need to make your tower as tall as possible. You can use only ten potatoes, but you can use as many plastic utensils as you like. Ready? You have ten minutes. Go!**

While groups work, offer help to anyone who's having trouble understanding the information on the handouts. Also, encourage kids to talk about their opinions and experiences regarding evolution and creationism. For example, ask:

● **What do you think about evolution? creationism?**
● **Have you ever had a debate with someone over this issue? Why or why not?**
● **Why do you think this issue seems so important to so many Christians?**
● **Is it important to you? Why or why not?**

Once time is up, say: **Today we're going to examine some tough questions about the beginning of the universe. Through our examination, we'll discover that no matter what you believe about how the world was created, the truth remains that <u>God created it.</u>**

Spud to Spud (up to 5 minutes)
Have kids each find a partner from the other group. Have pairs show off and explain their "theory towers" to their partners. Encourage kids to use the handouts or ask you for help in explaining the theories.

Once pairs finish their explanations, say: **Christians believe that <u>God created the universe.</u> But how he did it is up for debate. In fact, some of us in this room may have strong feelings about evolution or creationism. That's OK. But as we take a critical look at both of these theories, let's remember these "Lovin' Spud Guidelines":**
    1. Absolutely no personal put-downs.
    2. Strive first to understand, then to be understood.

3. Respect each other's right to an opinion, even if the opinion differs from yours.

Write these rules on newsprint, and tape them to the wall so kids can refer to them throughout the study.

UNITY PRAYER ▼

Spud Links (up to 5 minutes)

Say: **To start off our examination on the right foot, let's create a "spud link" of love between the groups.**

Give each person a potato and a marker. Say: **On your potato, write one word that represents something you value in your partner. For example, you might write "boldness" because your partner is outgoing. Once you're finished, explain what you wrote to your partner.**

When kids finish, have partners hold their potatoes between them and pray together. Encourage them to thank God for their partners and to ask God to teach them what he wants them to learn about evolution and creationism.

After the prayer time, have kids set their "love spuds" on the floor between the groups as a reminder to show love as they discuss evolution and creationism.

"Who put wisdom inside the mind or understanding in the heart?" — Job 38:36

DEPTHFINDER
THE THREE MEANINGS OF "EVOLUTION"

Evolution can be a confusing topic because the word can mean different things to different people. In this study, references to evolution refer to the scientific theory that "all the living forms in the world have arisen from a single source which itself came from an inorganic form." This is the theory of macroevolution.

Microevolution involves the proposition that "many living animals can be observed over the course of time to undergo changes so that new species are formed." Since this process can be demonstrated scientifically, it is considered a fact.

Both of these ideas differ from what many people call evolutionism, which isn't a scientific theory at all but a philosophy about the nature of life. Evolutionism promotes the idea that all life is constantly refining itself, moving "from lower to higher forms, leading to continued human improvement." Evolutionism carries its philosophy out of the scientific realm and applies it to all areas of life—including history, sociology, ethics, and religion. It is this philosophy—not so much the *scientific* theory of evolution—that has caused such a rift between faith and science on the issue of creation.

THEORY COLLAPSE ▼

Fallen Spuds (15 to 20 minutes)

Say: **Now we're ready to delve into the heart of this great controversy. You've built your theory, and now we're going to test it.**

Give the Evolutionists copies of the "Creationism—No!" handout (p. 24). Give the Creationists copies of the "Evolution—No!" handout (p. 24). Then say: **Your job is to try to collapse the other group's theory tower. Here's how you'll do it:**

1. Study your handout and look for evidence that goes against any argument used in the other group's theory tower.

2. Once you've compiled your evidence, you'll all take turns presenting the evidence to each other. If your opponents can't refute your evidence, they must remove from their tower the potato that corresponds to the argument you shot down.

3. We'll continue until both towers collapse or until time is up.

Once groups understand the rules, start the discussion.

DEBRIEFING ▼

This Spud's for You (10 to 15 minutes)

After fifteen minutes (or when both towers have collapsed), have kids return to the pairs they formed earlier in the study. Have pairs discuss these questions:

● **What's your reaction to this experience?**
● **What do you think about evolution now? creationism?**
● **How is this activity like having your beliefs attacked in real life?**
● **How is it similar to attacking someone else's beliefs?**

Have pairs read Genesis 1–2 and discuss:
● **Does this passage support either of the theories we've discussed? Why or why not?**
● **Does the Bible try to explain who created the universe? Why or why not?**
● **Does the Bible try to explain how <u>God created the universe</u>? Why or why not?**

Have pairs read Job 38:1-33, then discuss:
● **What does this passage say about the theory of evolution? the theory of creationism?**
● **When have you felt like Job in this passage?**
● **How should we respond when people challenge our beliefs about the origins of the universe?**
● **What could make you believe that <u>God created the universe</u>?**

Give each student a fresh potato and a marker. Say: **On your potato, write an answer to this question: "What quality in your partner makes you believe that <u>God created the universe?</u>"**

When kids finish, have them give their potatoes to their partners. Then say: **Take your potato home, and plant it as a reminder that you are the best evidence there is for showing that <u>God created the universe.</u>**

e v o l u t i o n — y e s !

EVOLUTION—YES!

Read the arguments below, then choose the ten you think are strongest. Write the number of each of your chosen arguments on a separate potato. Then use the plastic utensils and potatoes to create a tower that represents your theory.

Evolution is true because...

1 Scientists can organize all life on earth into categories of species, families, and orders. This suggests that all living things are related to each other, possibly through one common ancestor.

2 There are many skeletal similarities between different species, such as apes and humans or horses and elephants. This indicates an evolutionary relationship.

3 Embryos of many different kinds of animals look similar in the early stages of development. This suggests a common ancestor for all life forms.

4 All living organisms are composed of the same basic chemical substances.

5 Some types of plants and animals have appeared to undergo changes over time after being isolated from similar populations in other parts of the world. This change suggests that life evolves to adapt to changes in environment.

6 Unused organs in animals and people—for example, the appendix in humans—seem to represent "throwbacks" to an earlier stage of evolution when those organs were useful.

7 The fact that scientists can create new varieties of species by selectively breeding existing life forms indicates that the potential for evolution is possible.

8 The fact that mutations do occur in present-day species indicates that evolutionary change is possible. If a mutation turns out to be favorable, a whole new species may evolve.

9 The fossil record of the earth seems to indicate an evolutionary progression from ancient, simple organisms to more recent, complex organisms.

10 Many living organisms share common physiological traits, even though their species are supposedly unrelated.

11 Techniques used for dating fossils and rocks indicate that the earth is about 5 billion years old. This allows enough time for life to develop on earth according to evolutionary theory.

handout

ok to copy

creationism—yes!

CREATIONISM—YES!

Read the arguments below, then choose the ten you think are strongest. Write the number of each of your chosen arguments on a separate potato. Then use the plastic utensils and potatoes to create a tower that represents your theory.

Creationism is true because...

1 The laws of probability point to the existence of a Creator. For example, for even the simplest amino acid to have formed by chance, the earth would have to be at least twelve times older than scientists say it is. The fact that amino acids—which are the building blocks of life—exist at all, indicates an intelligent Creator.

2 The odds of a single strand of DNA forming by chance is about 1x10—followed by 147 zeros. That means the universe would have to be at least eighteen times older than scientists say in order for this possibility to occur.

3 Many deposits of fossil strata do not match the geologic column supported by evolutionary theory. Supposed older fossils are deposited directly on top of younger ones, with no evidence that the strata have been flipped.

4 Many formations in the world (such as the Grand Canyon) suggest that one or more cataclysmic events have occurred in earth's history. These events could account for the majority of the fossil record we see today.

5 Fossils can form only when organisms are buried so quickly that they have no time to decay or be eaten by scavengers. This fact seems to support the notion that a cataclysmic event—such as a worldwide flood—created the vast majority of fossils we see today.

6 Many archaeological discoveries support the notion of a cataclysmic event happening at some time in the past. For example, many animals in the Siberian wilderness have been discovered fully preserved, some still holding the food they were chewing when they suddenly perished. This suggests a cataclysmic event, not a series of "natural" deaths occurring over long periods of time.

7 The fossil record provides no evidence at all of gradual changes occurring to transform one species into another.

8 The fossil record only indicates the order in which various life forms were deposited. It doesn't indicate how much time passed between each deposit or how the deposits are related, if at all. Because of this, the record provides no evidence at all of any kind of gradual change from simpler to more complex organisms.

9 The Second Law of Thermodynamics states that anything which is organized tends, with time, to become disorganized. For this reason, our ordered universe could not have developed on its own from the chaos of the big bang. It must have had an organized Creator.

10 Life itself goes against the Second Law of Thermodynamics since it becomes more organized over time. This indicates an intelligent force that counteracts the natural forces of decay in the universe.

11 There is no scientific proof that life did (or even could) evolve into existence from inorganic matter. Conversely, there is abundant evidence to suggest that all life "comes from life"—that is, that life on earth was created by God.

EVOLUTION—NO!

Use these arguments (or some of your own) to try to collapse the other group's tower. The numbers assigned to the arguments below correspond to the numbers written on the tower.

1 Just because all life on earth has similarities doesn't mean it all evolved from a common ancestor. For example, all the houses on earth have certain similarities (roofs, walls, bedrooms, and so on), but they didn't all evolve from a single home sometime in the distant past. Houses are similar because they all have a similar function, and they're all created by an intelligence—just as all life was created by God.

5 This argument is about microevolution—that is, minor changes that happen within a species to help it adapt to a new environment. This is fact, and we don't deny it. But microevolution doesn't prove that macroevolution is true, any more than jumping over a ditch proves you can leap over the Grand Canyon.

8 Mutations that happen in nature are extremely rare. And of those that have been observed, about 99 percent of them are harmful to the species. The odds of getting enough "positive" mutations to create the diversity of life we see today are almost nil. In addition, even if a positive mutation did occur in some animal, how would it reproduce, unless another identical mutation happened at the same time?

11 Dating techniques for rocks and fossils depend on the assumption that the atmosphere and environment of the earth have been constant since the beginning of the world. Most scientists agree that such a constant state is unlikely since even today the nature of the atmosphere is constantly changing. So those dating techniques are unreliable.

CREATIONISM—NO!

Use these arguments (or some of your own) to try to collapse the other group's tower. The numbers assigned to the arguments below correspond to the numbers written on the tower.

5 Just because all fossils are created under cataclysmic circumstances doesn't prove they all died around the same time. Scientists observe animals and plants dying in cataclysmic ways every day. For example, animals die in flash floods, earthquakes, and other kinds of natural disasters.

7 No scientists believe the fossil record is complete as it is. Many gaps exist, which could explain why we see no evidence of gradual changes in species over time.

8 Scientific dating techniques give us the ability to date fossil and rock deposits, so we can tell how old they are, not just in what order they were laid down.

10 The fact that life grows more organized over time can be explained through the principle of natural selection and does not necessarily indicate the existence of God.

Reality Bites

WHY LIFE ISN'T PERFECT

---> by Karl Leuthauser ----

THE POINT:

Sin poisoned the world.

■ Your teenagers live in a world where their understanding of the truth is constantly challenged and changed. As comprehension is overthrown by confusion, disillusionment becomes kids' final line of defense. They have been disappointed by shrinking opportunities, an uncaring society, erratic friends, and shattered families. Without a stable knowledge of the truth, kids find themselves in the throes of discouragement—and desperate for hope. ■ Your young people need to know that they have an eternal and unshakable Advocate. More than ever, they must know that God is faithful and good, even when all else seems destined to disappoint them. ■ This study explores the reasons we experience disappointment and discouragement in a fallen world and demonstrates God's faithfulness and stability regardless of circumstance.

The Study
AT A GLANCE

SECTION	MINUTES	WHAT STUDENTS WILL DO	SUPPLIES
Warm-Up	10 to 15	NO FAIR SHARE—Share personal stories of discouragement, then pray.	
	5 to 10	THE DILEMMA—Read about God's goodness, then discuss why they feel let down so often.	Bibles
Investigative Study	20 to 25	POP GOES THE WORLD—Create a model of creation and demonstrate the effects of sin on the world.	Bibles, balloons, masking tape, markers, paper clips, "Pop Goes the World" handouts (p. 33), newsprint
Closing	10 to 15	IN WITH THE NEW—Create a reminder of hope to use in the future.	Bibles, balloons, index cards, markers, newsprint

notes:

THE POINT OF *REALITY BITES:*

Sin poisoned the world.

THE BIBLE CONNECTION

GENESIS 1:27-31	God is pleased with his creation of humanity.
GENESIS 3:16-19	God explains the consequences of the first sin.
NUMBERS 23:19 and 2 TIMOTHY 2:11-13	Unlike people, God is always faithful and true.
ROMANS 8:18-27	Christians and creation wait with excitement for God to redeem the world.

I n this study, kids will explore the reasons behind discouragement in their lives and make models of creation to examine how sin poisoned the world.

Through these experiences, kids can discover that discouragement stems from sin's initial entry into the world. They can find positive ways to deal with the disappointments they face and see the hope they can have even in the midst of discouraging circumstances.

Explore the verses in The Bible Connection, then examine the information in the Depthfinder boxes throughout the study to gain a deeper understanding of how these Scriptures connect with your young people.

THE STUDY

LEADER TIP for The Study

Because this topic can be so powerful and relevant to kids' lives, your group members may be tempted to get caught up in issues and lose sight of the deeper biblical principle found in The Point. Help your kids grasp The Point by guiding kids to focus on the biblical investigations and discussing how God's truth connects with reality in their lives.

WARM-UP ▼

No Fair Share (10 to 15 minutes) As kids arrive, have them form groups of three. After they've had a chance to say hello, say: **For the next few minutes, I want you to share with your group the most discouraging thing that has ever happened in your life. Everyone in the group must share a story. If you don't want to share your worst disappointment, share one that you're comfortable telling others. While you**

LEADER TIP

for Pop Goes the World

To help kids focus, give them the instructions before you distribute the materials. When you hold the materials, the kids will look at you and listen to you. When they hold the materials, they'll focus on the materials.

DEPTH FINDER — TRUTH, LIES, AND DISCOURAGEMENT

Emotions are one of the most volatile and dominant aspects of the teenage years. Kids find it difficult to separate what they know from what they feel. When parents, teachers, or other trusted authority figures disappoint them, kids feel intensely frustrated, angry, and insecure. They may direct these feelings toward God. Kids may feel that God also is unjust, unkind, or simply apathetic.

Kids need to know that God remains faithful—even when they're faithless (2 Timothy 2:13). God will always support them, even when they can't feel his presence (Psalm 121). He has made that promise in his Word (Proverbs 30:5).

As you explore discouragement in kids' lives, encourage them to recognize that when God seems to be unapproachable or distant, they can boldly go before him to find mercy and compassion (Hebrews 4:16).

share, include how you felt and how you reacted to the discouraging situation.

When kids appear to be wrapping it up, say: **Many of us have gone through some pretty discouraging circumstances. Anger, embarrassment, and sadness are appropriate responses to disappointment. However, if you felt angry while you were telling your story, you may need to forgive someone who disappointed you. If you felt embarrassed, you may need to forgive yourself. If you felt sad, you may need God to touch your sorrow.**

Have kids stay in their groups and take a moment to pray for one another. Encourage kids to ask God to show them any disappointment that still needs to be dealt with. If some kids say that they don't have any discouragement in their lives, encourage them to use this time to pray for friends or family.

The Dilemma (5 to 10 minutes)

When kids finish praying, gather everyone together and ask:
● **Based on what you shared in your trios, what kinds of things make you feel discouraged?**

Have volunteers read Numbers 23:19 and 2 Timothy 2:11-13 aloud. Say: **God is faithful even when we aren't. He's always in control and does what he says he will do. He never disappoints us, and he never causes us to be discouraged.** Then ask:
● **Since God is so faithful and true, why do we feel let down so often?**

Allow a few minutes of discussion, then say: **That is a difficult question. We often blame God for discouragement in our lives. But through this study, we'll discover that God never intended us to feel discouraged or disappointed. Instead, discouragement is caused by <u>sin, which has poisoned the world.</u>**

Pop Goes the World

(20 to 25 minutes)

Say: **You're going to look at the main reason for the discouragement and disappointment that people face. You'll need to do this next activity with the people that were in your prayer group. After you get back into your group, have one of your group members come and get one balloon, one strip of masking tape, one paper clip, a few markers, and one handout for each person in your group.**

After each group has the necessary materials, instruct groups to follow the directions on their "Pop Goes the World" handouts (p. 33).

While groups complete the handouts, write the following questions on newsprint, and tape it to a wall:

● How did you feel when your model was poked?

● If you had made the most beautiful thing ever created, how would you feel about watching someone ruin it?

● How is the paper clip like sin?

● How is it different?

● According to Genesis 3:16-19, what's the result of Adam and Eve's sin?

LEADER TIP

for Pop Goes the World

To save time, you may want to separate the materials and set them on a table before the study begins.

LEADER TIP

for Pop Goes the World

When kids poke the balloons, some of the balloons may pop and some of them may leak air. If this happens, don't worry. The debriefing questions that follow this activity will work no matter what happens to the balloons.

DEPTH FINDER — ACTIVELY SEARCHING FOR HOPE

"Close to 50 percent of kids come from divorced families. Many are latchkey kids, who come home from school to an empty house and fend for themselves."
—Dieter Zander, "The Gospel for Generation X," Christianity Today magazine, 1995

"Two-thirds of the more than 14 million recipients of Aid to Families with Dependent Children...are sixteen or younger."
—Editorial page, USA Today, September 21, 1995

"Thirty-two percent of teens say drugs are their biggest problem."
—Editorial page, USA Today, July 18, 1995

"Violence occurs in nearly one-third of all high school– and college-age dating relationships."
—"Dangerous Liaisons," Sassy magazine, March 1996

Today's kids have plenty to be discouraged about. Those kids in your group who are the most difficult to reach are probably the ones who most need to hear about God's love. They may have been disappointed, displaced, distanced, and downplayed so often that they won't risk hoping that you really care about them. You have the opportunity to demonstrate God's hope to them—a hope that says, "No matter how much you roll your eyes or complain, and no matter how you act, I still want you here."

There are several practical ways you can show this hope to kids in your group. For example, you can pray with your kids individually, actively listen to them, or involve them in leadership roles. Whatever you do, make sure you show your kids that you're not put off by their outward actions. Let your kids know that you're genuinely interested in them and that you'd like everyone to participate because you value everyone's input.

UNDERSTANDING THE BIBLE

You get what you deserve...

We've all heard the phrase. We all know what it means. But is it true? Not according to the Bible.

Sometimes our sin leads directly to being discouraged. But the Bible clearly states that many of our personal disappointments have little or nothing to do with our actions. They're a result of living in a fallen world. In John 9:1-3, Jesus tells his followers that it was neither the blind man's sin nor his parents' sin that caused him to be blind at birth. In fact, God had a purpose for the man's ailment. God used it to bring glory to himself.

Some of your kids may think that discouraging circumstances are punishments for sin in their own lives. Help them to realize that all people experience suffering and disappointment—simply because we all live in a sin-poisoned world.

● Based on that same passage, what's the ultimate cause of discouragement in our lives?

After kids finish the handouts, say: **I'd like you to discuss within your group the questions on the newsprint. Be prepared to share your group's ideas with everyone else when you're finished.**

When groups finish their discussions, gather everyone together and ask:

● **What, ultimately, is the cause of discouragement in our lives?**

● **What does the Bible say about the question "Since God is faithful and true, why do we get let down so often?"**

After kids have shared their answers, say: **God created a world that was perfect beyond the greatest balloon model ever made. Sin did more than get Adam and Eve kicked out of the Garden of Eden. <u>Sin poisoned everything and everyone in God's perfect world.</u> It is at the root of all the discouragement in our lives.**

CLOSING ▼

In With the New (10 to 15 minutes)
Say: **Knowing why we get discouraged isn't enough. We still need to figure out how to handle discouragement when it comes. Ask: Based on your experience, what's the best way to deal with discouragement?**

Once several kids have responded, distribute index cards, and say: **We're going to take some time to look at the directions God gives us for dealing with discouragement. On the index card I've given you, write the following verses: Psalm 42:5-6; Jeremiah 29:11-13; John 14:1-4; and James 1:2-4.**

Take a minute to read each passage and discover what God says about dealing with discouragement. On your index card,

"We know that *everything* God made has been waiting until now in pain, like a woman ready to give birth. Not only the world, but we also have been waiting with pain inside us. We have the Spirit as the first part of *God's promise.* So we are waiting for God to finish making us his own children, which means our bodies will be made free."
—Romans 8:22-23

DEPTHFINDER — UNDERSTANDING THESE KIDS

For many kids, discouragement is real and immediate. They may not understand how Christ's return has anything to do with their present circumstances. As you explain the verses of hope found in this study, encourage kids with the truth that discouragement has as much to do with how we look at disappointment as it has to do with the disappointment itself. Help them see that God doesn't offer life without disappointment, but he does offer life with a different perspective—a perspective that enables us to see immediate circumstances from an eternal viewpoint.

write your discoveries.

While kids work, write these questions on newsprint, and tape it to a wall:

● Why do you think this passage instructs us to hope in God's redemption?

● How does hoping in God help you deal with discouragement?

When kids finish, have them each turn to a partner and read together Romans 8:18-27. Then have pairs discuss the questions you listed on newsprint.

As pairs wrap up their discussions, give each person a new balloon. Say: **Take the index card with the verses about dealing with discouragement, and put it inside the balloon I just gave you. After you get it inside the balloon, blow up the balloon, then tie it off.**

While the kids follow your instructions, set markers in the middle of the room. Say: **Using the markers and your balloons, describe what the world will be like when Jesus returns and we no longer have reasons for discouragement. Use words or phrases such as "peace" or "no more hunger" to demonstrate the difference.**

When the kids finish, say: **I'd like you to take your balloon home with you. If you feel discouraged in the next week, pop the balloon, and look at the passages you've written. If the balloon deflates before you need to pop it, take out the card and read the passages. Then thank God for bringing you through the week without discouragement. Thank him for giving us hope in a fallen world.**

POP GOES THE WORLD

 1 Blow up your balloon, and tie it off.

 2 Put the strip of masking tape on the balloon anywhere above the knot.

 3 Using the markers and your balloon, create a model of what a perfect world would look like from space.

 4 Read Genesis 1:27-31. How is the model you made like God's creation? How is it different?

 5 Genesis 1:27 says that God created us in his image. Tell the person on your left one way that you see God's image in him or her.

 6 Within your group, pass your model to the person on your left.

 7 Straighten out the paper clip, and poke one end through the masking tape on the model you're holding.

 8 Pull out the paper clip, and observe what happens.

 9 Read Genesis 3:16-19.

what a wonderful world

CATCHING A GLIMPSE OF GOD'S MAJESTY

by Mikal Keefer

THE POINT:

God's creation surpasses our imagination.

■ The award for The Most Amazing Invention is about to be presented, so gather around. Behold the winner. It slices. It dices. It does julienne fries. It's *you*, warts and all. Your body is an amazing creation. According to *Today's World: The Human Body...* ■ *It's an amazing feat of engineering and biology. This "machine" is a complex collection of 100 trillion cells that somehow all work together.* ■ *It's strong enough to push a VW out of a ditch and flexible enough to pick up a single grain of sand. This "invention" boasts seven hundred skeletal muscles that put the most sophisticated robots to shame.* ■ *It's able to convert almost anything (including chili burritos) into fuel. It features the world's most impressive data processing equipment in the form of a three-pound blob sitting between two ears. Standard equipment includes state-of-the-art, instant-focus cameras; full auditory input sensors; a twenty-six-foot digestive system; and much, much more!* ■ And you're just one of the many mysterious and beautiful aspects of God's creation. God's attention to detail can be found in every living thing. His limitlessness and power can be seen by looking up at the sky. As kids look at the wonders that God has created, they'll have no choice but to see the beauty, majesty, and mystery of the Creator.

What a Wonderful World

The Study
AT A GLANCE

SECTION	MINUTES	WHAT STUDENTS WILL DO	SUPPLIES
Travel Game	10 to 15	MYSTERY TOURS—Identify mysterious places in God's creation and convince others to go there.	Index cards, pencils
Creative Investigation	15 to 20	HOOP INSPECTIONS—Focus on a section of God's creation and discuss what it communicates about God.	Bibles, wire coat hangers, "Hoop Dreams" handout (p. 42), pencils
Creative Expression	10 to 15	THE MUGGING OF AN ALIEN—Mime an event of the human immune system.	"The Key Players" handout (p. 43), cardboard box, scissors
	10 to 15	PSALM PSELECTIONS—Investigate a psalm, create their own psalms, and pray.	Bibles, paper, pencils, "Where Are They Now?" Depthfinder (p. 41)

notes:

THE POINT OF *WHAT A WONDERFUL WORLD:*

God's creation surpasses our imagination.

THE BIBLE CONNECTION

PSALM 8:3-8	God makes people rulers of his creation.
PSALMS 19:1-6 and 148	God's creation is a constant testimony of his existence and glory.

I n this study, kids will create and "sell" tours of mysterious destinations in God's creation, focus on small areas of creation, investigate the complexity of life, and respond to God's work by creating their own psalms and prayers.

By doing this, kids can discover that God is praiseworthy and powerful and that he has made himself evident through his creation. They can also discover that they have value because they were created by God.

Explore the verses in The Bible Connection, then examine the information in the Depthfinder boxes throughout the study to gain a deeper understanding of how these Scriptures connect with your young people.

THE STUDY

LEADER TIP for The Study

Because this topic can be so powerful and relevant to kids' lives, your group members may be tempted to get caught up in issues and lose sight of the deeper biblical principle found in The Point. Help your kids grasp The Point by guiding them to focus on the biblical investigation and discussing how God's truth connects with reality in their lives.

TRAVEL GAME ▼

Mystery Tours (10 to 15 minutes) As kids arrive, have them form pairs. Give each pair an index card and a pencil. Then say: **Congratulations, almost-graduates of the** (name of your church) **Travel Agent Academy. You've completed the course work required for your diploma, but you still need to complete your senior project.**

DEPTHFINDER
A BONUS IDEA

For a special activity, ask a parent to bring a very young child to your meeting and to place the baby in just a diaper where your teenagers can see him or her. Ask your teenagers to gather around the child without actually touching him or her. Then ask the parent to show his or her own baby picture.

Ask:

● **What features of the baby remind you of this parent?**

● **What features of creation remind you of its Creator?**

● **When you stop and look at a new baby, what's the most amazing thing about it? Why?**

● **In what ways do humans remind you of our Creator?**

Close by thanking the parent and saying: **God's creation surpasses our imagination!**

You must design your own Mystery Tour.

To design your tour, think of a natural place that's wonderful and mysterious. You can go down the mouth of an erupting volcano or inside a sunflower. You can be any size you want, and you don't have to worry about oxygen, heat, cold, or other discomforts. You have three minutes to jot down reasons your tour location is wonderful and mysterious and the reasons others would want to go there. As you work, keep in mind that you'll be asked to give a thirty-second infomercial designed to sell your travel destination to others.

Give pairs about three minutes to work. Then say: **It's now time for your infomercials. Each group will give a thirty-second infomercial. During your infomercial, try to sell your destination to others by explaining where they'd go and what they'd see.**

Give each of the pairs an opportunity to present its infomercial to the rest of the class. Make certain to limit the presentations to thirty seconds. Commend students for their efforts and creativity.

Then say: **Your tours were very interesting. But as unique as the locations are, they have one thing in common: God's creative work is evident in them all.**

Then ask:

● **What did you find amazing about the location you chose?**

● **What did you find amazing about the other locations?**

● **What do the locations tell you about the Creator?**

Say: **Think about the most impressive things people have created. Think about the amazing things people have accomplished. What's even more incredible is that God created the minds of those people who created such things. The more we look at God's creation, the more we see his mystery and beauty. He's an amazing Creator and <u>his creation surpasses our imagination.</u>**

CREATIVE INVESTIGATION ▼

Hoop Inspections (15 to 20 minutes)

Have kids form groups of four. Give each group a wire coat hanger, a "Hoop Dreams" handout (p. 42), and a pencil. Make certain each group has a Bible. Lead the groups to as "natural" a spot as the environment and schedule allow.

Ask the groups to spread out and stretch their wire coat hangers into circles. Ask the groups to toss their hoops at least ten feet in front of them. Have the groups investigate the areas where their circles land by completing their handouts. When all groups have finished their handouts, lead them back to your meeting room.

Say: **We've found so much in such small places, but think of what we'd find if our hoops had landed on Venus or in the Amazon. God's creation is truly spectacular. It's so massive and intricate. His creation surpasses our imagination.**

LEADER TIP for Hoop Inspections

If time permits, close this activity by having kids read Psalm 139:14-16.

CREATIVE EXPRESSION ▼

The Mugging of an Alien (10 to 15 minutes)

Say: **Much of God's most amazing work happens where we can't see it. It happens light-years from here, under ground, or even inside our bodies. Let's take a look at a common but amazing occurrence that's going on inside you right now.**

Set a cardboard box in the middle of the room. (The larger the box, the better.) Have kids form four groups. Distribute one of the roles from "The Key Players" handout (p. 43) to each group. Have groups decide how they'll mime the parts described on the handout and wait for you to call them into action "on stage." Explain that the cardboard box symbolizes the tissue cell you will refer to in your story. Tell the groups to mime the action as you read the following story and allow time for groups to act out what you read.

The Mugging of an Alien

As Lenny lay sleeping, he knew nothing of the internal conflict that was soon to occur. Within the many cells of Lenny's body, a single tissue cell (point to the box) located in Lenny's throat was about to be attacked. Lenny's plasma busily directed red blood cells to the tissue cell. Once there, the red blood cells delivered oxygen to the tissue cell. Then the plasma sent the empty-handed red blood cells back to the lungs to pick up more oxygen. This cycle continued during the assault that followed.

As the red blood cells were making their second trip, an influenza virus mixed in with the crowd. The virus was tired. It had been looking for a place to call home.

LEADER TIP for Hoop Inspections

If weather or limited time prevents you from going outside your meeting room, give each group a nature photo from National Geographic, Arizona Highways, or other travel magazines to use as their areas of investigation.

If magazines aren't available, you can spin a globe, and ask a representative from each group to close his or her eyes and pinpoint a location by stopping the spinning globe with his or her finger. That location will be the team's area of inspection. If too many teams pinpoint oceans, you can have them inspect countries that are nearest to their fingers. Tell kids to imagine what they'd find in that country to answer the questions on the handout.

DEPTH FINDER

IT'S ALL IN THERE

As your teenagers discuss the mysteries of God's creation, you can add to the conversation by offering the following facts:

● There are 206 bones in an adult body.

● If you stretched out your small intestines, they'd be between twenty and thirty feet long.

● Each of your eyeballs has six small, slim muscles connected to it.

● The average tongue has ten thousand taste buds.

The plasma simply did its job and directed the virus to the tissue cell. The virus found the cell to be satisfactory and set up its home. As the virus settled in, it grew and multiplied. Red blood cells continued to deliver oxygen to the tissue cell that was beginning to be overcome by its unwelcome guests.

The tissue cell was becoming so overcrowded that it was on the verge of exploding. Lenny's tissue cell was headed for certain disaster. Suddenly, the plasma found that it was directing white blood cells to the scene. Reinforcements continued to arrive. The white blood cells surrounded the virus, and engulfed it. The virus had been defeated, and Lenny continued to sleep.

Give all your actors a round of applause. Have teenagers form groups of three and discuss the following questions:

● **How do different blood cells know what to do?**

● **If you were designing a defense system for your body, would you do anything differently? If so, what?**

● **What does the design of our bodies tell us about our Creator?**

Say: **When God created us, he knew what he was doing. You're made in a wonderful way. The detail of your body and the complexity of how you work is amazing. You, like the rest of God's creation, surpass imagination.**

Psalm Pselections (10 to 15 minutes)

Give each group paper and a pencil. Say: **I'd like you to read Psalm 148 with your group. After you read it, make a list of some of the things that God has made that you think are amazing and interesting.**

When groups finish their lists, say: **I'd like you to create your own psalms that praise God for what he has made. Include one statement about each of your group members. For example, you might write, "Praise you, God, for making Kyle; you've given him such a great smile." Also try to incorporate the amazing and interesting things from your lists.**

Give groups about five minutes to prepare their psalms. Have the entire group form a circle. Say: **We're going to pray a prayer of praise. Each person needs to pray about one thing in God's creation that he or she is especially thankful for. You can use verses**

from your psalms if you like. However, if your verse will distract from praising God, please don't read it.

Explain that you'll begin the prayer and that the prayer will move to your right. Start by saying: **God, thank you for your <u>creation that surpasses our imagination.</u> I thank you for this group and the creativity you've given them.**

Encourage kids to continue the prayer until the person on your left has had a chance to pray. As kids leave, give each of them a copy of the "Where Are They Now?" Depthfinder (below).

DEPTHFINDER WHERE ARE THEY NOW?

In the ancient world there were feats of engineering and building that were deemed so impressive that they were heralded as the "Seven Wonders of the World." They were:

● **Artemision at Ephesus** was a temple to the Greek goddess Artemis. It took 220 years to complete. In A.D. 262 a group of very annoyed Goths destroyed it.

● **The Colossus of Rhodes** was one hundred feet tall, bronze, and built to overlook a harbor. This statue of the sun god Helios was erected in about 280 B.C. and was toppled by an earthquake around 224 B.C. In A.D. 653 the remains were sold as scrap metal.

● **The Hanging Gardens of Babylon** were a series of five terraces, each fifty feet above the next. King Nebuchadnezzar gave them to his wife as a gift. A winding stairway connected the five levels, and special fountains irrigated rare and exotic plants. None of it remains.

● **The Mausoleum at Halicarnassus** was built in 352 B.C. This 140-foot-high white marble structure housed the tomb of King Mausolus of Caria. In 1402, St. John's men destroyed it to get stone to build a castle.

● **Olympian Zeus** was a statue made of gold, marble, and ivory. It was forty feet tall and rested on a base that was twelve feet high and sat in the temple at Olympia. Unfortunately, it's been misplaced.

● **The Tower of Pharos** was a lighthouse built in 285 B.C. It was five hundred feet tall and emitted the light of a fire, boosted with reflectors, that could be seen for forty-two miles. But it no longer exists.

● **The Pyramids of Egypt** are all that's left of the Seven Wonders of the World.

Humans have created and achieved many impressive things. Some people point to our advancements as proof of our ability to be self-sufficient. Some people use them to support the theory that we will eventually evolve into god-like status.

It's important to remember that like the Seven Wonders of the World, *all* of our material accomplishments will be lost, forgotten, or destroyed. When we die, or when Jesus returns, our love and adoration for him as acted out in love and support of others is the only accomplishment we'll have to show for our lives.

hoop dreams

1. Make a list of every living thing you see within your area.

_____

_____

_____

2. Make a list of all the nonliving things within your area.

_____

_____

_____

3. Make a list of all the things within your area that were created by God.

_____

_____

_____

4. Make a list of all the things within your area that were created by people.

_____

_____

_____

Discuss and answer the following questions:

● What did you find in your area that qualifies as "amazing"?

● What's your best guess as to what's about a mile under your area? a mile above it?

● What do you think filled this spot a hundred years ago? a thousand years ago?

● What do you think will fill this spot in a hundred years? a thousand years?

● What does your little section of creation say about the Creator?

● What's the most amazing thing you can think of that's in God's creation that could fit into your circle?

● Read Psalm 19:1-6. How does what you see in your list of items reflect God's glory?

● If you were the Creator, what would you change about what's in your area?

● Read Psalm 8:3-8. How have humans honored or dishonored the Creator's mandate that we be caretakers of your little section?

the key players

Red Blood Cells

Your job is to swim around, carrying loads of oxygen to other cells, who gratefully receive your gifts of life. You bring oxygen to areas of the body then drop it off. You leave to pick up more oxygen and return to drop it off again.

- -

White Blood Cells

You're the army of the body. You circulate through the bloodstream on patrol, looking for invaders who might hurt the body.
When you spot a villain, you surround and destroy it, usually by eating it or engulfing it. You take no prisoners.

- -

Plasma

You make sure all the other blood cells get where they're going. You're the bloodstream's traffic directors. You don't get involved in fights, you don't carry anything yourself, and you don't really care who's going where. Your goal is to keep deliveries on time and moving along.

- -

Viruses

You don't want to be mean, but you have to look out for yourself. You're very imperialistic, and you're loyal to your own kind. You're willing to do just about anything to increase your territory and numbers. You're passed along through the air or through touch until you find a place to call home. You attach to your host cell by burrowing into it. You grow and multiply within the cell until there is no room left and the host cell explodes.

Reduce, Renew, Respond

BRINGING THE GREEN FULL CIRCLE

by Debbie Gowensmith and Helen Turnbull

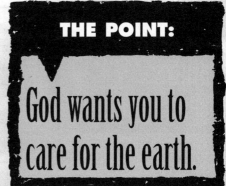

THE POINT:

God wants you to care for the earth.

■ Smog. Water pollution. Deforestation. Animal extinction. ■ Your teenagers hear every day about environmental concerns—in school, on TV, in their music, and in their communities. ■ The result? Ninety-one percent of teenagers say they're personally concerned with environmental problems (*America's Youth in the 1990s*, The George H. Gallup International Institute). But your kids may be getting confusing messages: that a mythological idol governs the earth; that nature itself—instead of its Creator—deserves worship; that their Christian faith and their concern for the environment are fundamentally opposed. ■ You can expose the myths and help your kids walk in the truth. With sound biblical backing, you can teach your kids that God created the earth and entrusted humanity to care for it. You can encourage them to worship God for his gift of the earth and demonstrate that they can be trusted with such a valuable gift. And you can show them how basic Christian principles such as outreach, stewardship, and servanthood can guide their concerns for God's creation. With these messages, you can help your kids discover that caring for God's creation *is* a Christian action.

The Study
AT A GLANCE

SECTION	MINUTES	WHAT STUDENTS WILL DO	SUPPLIES
Eye-Opener	10 to 15	HANDLE WITH CARE—Pass eggs using their elbows and discuss the fragility of creation.	Bibles, raw eggs, "Green Wars" handouts (p. 55), rags
Creative Exploration and Application	10 to 15	ECO-ART—Create a mural and discuss creation as God's gift to us.	Bibles, tape, newsprint, markers
	15 to 20	DOWN TO EARTH—Apply Christian principles to environmental problems.	Bibles, newsprint, markers, pencils, magazines, scissors, glue
Positive Reinforcement	10 to 15	REDUCE, RENEW, REJOICE—Run a relay that demonstrates the differences individuals can make.	Aluminum cans, cardboard box, newsprint, marker

notes:

THE POINT OF *REDUCE, RENEW, RESPOND:*

God wants you to care for the earth.

THE BIBLE CONNECTION

GENESIS 1	God creates the earth and entrusts it and everything in it to humanity.
PSALMS 92:1-5 and 104:1-24	The psalmists praise God for his creation and works.
MATTHEW 28:19-20	Jesus tells the disciples to spread God's message.
MARK 9:35	Jesus tells the disciples to be servants to others.
LUKE 12:48	Jesus explains that responsibility comes with his blessings.
1 CORINTHIANS 4:1-2	Paul encourages Christians to be faithful with what they're given.

I n this study, kids will play a game to learn how they handle fragile items, create a mural that represents God's gift of creation, use Christian principles to respond to an environmental problem, and run a relay to witness the difference that both individuals and groups can make.

Through these activities, kids can learn that God created the earth and wants us to care for his creation. They can discover that with Christian principles to guide them, they can improve what may seem like overwhelming environmental problems.

Explore the verses in The Bible Connection, then examine the information in the Depthfinder boxes throughout the study to gain a deeper understanding of how these Scriptures connect with your young people.

BEFORE THE STUDY

Gather ten clean aluminum cans for every four students in your group. Make one photocopy of the "Green Wars" handout (p. 55) for every four people in your group.

Write the word "recycling" on a cardboard box that's large enough to hold all the cans. Write the following statistic on a sheet of newsprint:

"Recycling one aluminum can saves the energy equivalent of about eight gallons of gasoline" ("50 Simple Things You Can Do to Save the Earth").

LEADER TIP
for The Study

If you need help collecting cans, ask kids to bring some from home. Or set up a box in your meeting room a couple of weeks before you use this study. Have kids and other church members deposit aluminum cans from home or church in the box.

If you still have difficulty gathering enough cans for all your students, just collect one can per student and revise the "Reduce, Renew, Rejoice" activity according to the Leader Tip on page 53.

THE STUDY

EYE-OPENER ▼

Handle With Care

(10 to 15 minutes)

After kids arrive, have them form teams of four. Give each team a raw egg, and ask the teams to form small circles. Say: **I'll give you forty-five seconds to see how many times your team can pass your raw egg around the circle without breaking it. The team whose egg completes the most circles wins. There is a catch, though: You have to pass the egg using only your elbows. If you break the egg, your whole team has to sit down—and guess who gets to clean up the mess? Ready? Go!**

After about forty-five seconds, call time, and encourage kids to help each other clean up any messes. Then ask:

● **How did you handle the eggs in this game? Why?**

● **How would this game be different if, instead of raw eggs, you used wads of paper?**

● **Is the way you handled the eggs like the way you should handle all fragile things? Why or why not?**

● **If God gave you a special, fragile gift, how would you handle it?**

Have teams read aloud Genesis 1. Then have teams discuss these questions:

● **What does this passage tell you about creation? about the earth? about God?**

● **When God looked at what he had created, what was his evaluation?**

● **According to this Scripture, who does the earth belong to, and who was entrusted with it?**

● **According to this Scripture, is the earth a gift from God? Why or why not?**

Give each team a photocopy of the "Green Wars" handout (p. 55), and have team members take turns reading the different arguments. Then have teams discuss each argument, citing things in each box they agree and disagree with. After a few minutes of discussion, read aloud 1 Corinthians 4:1-2. Ask:

● **What does this passage say about God's trust?**

● **If God entrusted you with something valuable and fragile, how do you think he would want you to care for it?**

● **How do you think God wants us to treat the earth?**

● **Are we treating the earth the way God wants us to? Why or why not?**

Say: **God created this complex and fragile earth from nothing. After he finished each element of his creation, he paused to appreciate it. When God's masterpiece was finally finished, he gave humanity the responsibility for everything in it. God wants**

<u>us to care for the earth,</u> his fragile creation, and it's up to us to rise to the occasion.

CREATIVE EXPLORATION AND APPLICATION ▼

Eco-Art (10 to 15 minutes) Tape a long, wide piece of newsprint to a wall, and scatter colorful markers below the newsprint. Say: **To understand our great responsibility for God's creation, let's take a minute to acknowledge and appreciate God for the earth. In Psalm 104, a poet expresses wonder and amazement for God's wisdom and power as he surveys God's creation.**

LEADER TIP for Eco-Art

To keep the study flowing, set up the relay elements for the "Reduce, Renew, Rejoice" activity while kids draw.

LEADER TIP for The Study

Whenever groups discuss a list of questions, write the list on newsprint, and tape it to the wall so groups can move through the discussion at their own pace.

DEPTH FINDER — UNDERSTANDING GENESIS

In his book, *A Worldly Spirituality: The Call to Redeem Life on Earth*, Wesley Granberg-Michaelson explains how the book of Genesis is often misinterpreted. The verses below are often used to support the modern assumption that humanity's exploitation of nature is justified. Granberg-Michaelson maintains that in historical context, exactly the opposite is intended.

Genesis 1:27-28

Many take God's instruction for man to "subdue the earth" as divine license to use creation to one's advantage and profit. Granberg-Michaelson argues: "Dominion in Genesis means that humanity is given the Godly responsibility of upholding and protecting the life of the animal world, and to do so on God's behalf...The 'subduing' carried out by humanity is to have a positive function, upholding the order and intention of God's creation."

Genesis 2:8-15

That God planted the Garden of Eden suggests that creation was provided to sustain the living environment necessary for man. Yet verse 15 says that God put Adam in the garden "to till it and keep it" (Revised Standard Version). Granberg-Michaelson notes that the Hebrew word for till is "abad" and means "serve," or even "being a slave to." The Hebrew word for "keep" is "shamar," which can mean "to watch or preserve."

Genesis 3:15-19

These verses are often quoted to support the idea that God put a "curse" on the earth and that humanity should therefore avoid caring for it. But Granberg-Michaelson shows how this curse is only a result of humanity's attempt to be like God rather than live in the image of God. Granberg-Michaelson says: "Rather than preserving all life, humanity believes it can take life into its own hands; in the chapter that follows, Cain kills Abel. And rather than regard the life of creation as God's gift, humanity now tries to act as though it owns the creation."

Granberg-Michaelson acknowledges the book of Genesis as God's covenant with creation. He views humanity as having an interdependence with creation and a relationship of harmony. Only when humanity rebels against God or his creation is this interdependent harmony disrupted.

In each team, have kids take turns reading Psalm 104:1-24. Then say: **Using that Scripture for inspiration, let's create a mural to show God how much we appreciate the gift of his creation. You can draw pictures or write poems or descriptions—even mathematical equations. Just express thanks to God for those things in creation that you admire most. You have a couple of minutes.**

After five minutes, gather the kids in front of the mural. Have everyone describe how his or her contribution to the mural represents God's incredible gifts. Congratulate the group on a beautiful creation. Then ask:

- **What does our creative effort say about God's creation?**
- **How does our mural compare with God's creative efforts?**
- **How was creating your mural like creating the universe?**
- **How do you think God felt as he looked upon his new creation of the world?**

Say: **The Bible says that at the end of each day of creation, God looked upon what he'd accomplished and saw that it was good.** Ask:

- **How do you think God wants us to treat his creation?**
- **Why are some Christians opposed to environmentalism?**

Say: **Verse 24 of the psalm we just read says, "Lord, you have made many things; with your wisdom you made them all. The earth is full of your riches." Our mural represents God's riches and can remind us that <u>God wants us to care for the earth.</u>**

Down to Earth (15 to 20 minutes)

Have kids form four groups. Assign each group one of the following Christian principles and Scriptures:

1) servanthood—Mark 9:35
2) outreach—Matthew 28:19-20
3) thankfulness—Psalm 92:1-5
4) stewardship—Luke 12:48

In each group, have a volunteer read his or her group's Scripture aloud. Then have each group discuss the following questions:

- **How do your verses apply to caring for God's creation?**
- **How does your principle apply to environmental issues?**
- **Based on your Christian principle, how do you think God would want you to address an environmental problem?**

Say: **<u>God wants you to care for the earth.</u> Based on our Christian principles, let's see how we can respond to an environmental concern such as water pollution. In your groups, discuss some of the problems with water pollution. Then identify a specific problem that leads to water pollution that your Christian principle could address, and come up with a contribution you could make that's based on your Christian principle. For example, if "servanthood" is your Christian principle, you could identify the problem of trash on the banks of a river. Because God wants us to use our faith to serve him and other people, your contribution could be spending a Saturday picking up trash that would otherwise pollute God's creation and the community's water supply. By volunteering your time, you'd be serving the whole community.**

LEADER TIP for Down to Earth

If your community is dealing with a more prominent environmental issue, you may want to focus on it as a teachable moment during this activity. Not only will this get your kids excited about the activity, it will also provide a clearer link between their faith and environmental concerns.

Hand each group a sheet of newsprint. Place markers, pencils, magazines, scissors, and glue in the middle of the room. Say: **After you've decided how to apply your principle, I'd like you to create the front page of a newspaper that shows the difference acting out your principle would make in the community. You can use the magazines to find photos to glue to your front page, or you can draw the pictures. Create a cover article that explains how your principle was put into action. You can also create surrounding articles that explain related details and events.**

Give kids about ten minutes to brainstorm and create their front pages. When they've finished, have each group present its front page to the class. Then ask:

● **What did this activity tell you about your faith and God's creation? about Christianity and God's creation? about Christianity and environmentalism?**

● **Did this activity change the way you'll approach concerns about God's creation? If so, how? If not, why not?**

● **What Christian principle could you use during the next couple of weeks to act on an environmental concern?**

Have kids remain in their groups. Ask them to pray for the environment

LEADER TIP
for Down to Earth

To further demonstrate the principle of outreach, let kids display their front pages throughout the church after class. They'll love to show off what they've learned and created, and the front pages could serve as interesting discussion starters.

DEPTH FINDER UNDERSTANDING THESE KIDS

"**M**ost teen-agers are very concerned about the environment, both throughout the world and in their own country and community. They do not feel enough progress is being made to protect and restore the environment, and the great majority would willingly enlist in the cause to reverse the trends" (*America's Youth in the 1990s*, The George H. Gallup International Institute).

The road from ideal to action, however, is not as well-traveled. Kids' environmental enthusiasm can be short-lived. As researcher George Barna wrote in *Generation Next*, "[The state of the environment] lurks in their minds as a looming disaster over which they may have no control or contribution." And that, say some researchers, is exactly what breeds apathy. When people feel overwhelmed, hopeless, and ineffective, they tend to give up (*Ecopsychology*, Roszak, et al).

Focusing on positive strides and personal efforts, no matter how seemingly small, talking with other people about their successes, and taking time to acknowledge and appreciate even methodical steps can provide tremendous boosts (*Ecopsychology*). In fact, a survey of Michigan educators revealed that the best teaching strategies in environmental education include case studies of success stories and talking about what others do to solve environmental problems (Martha C. Monroe and Stephen Kaplan, "When Words Speak Louder Than Actions: Environmental Problem Solving in the Classroom," Journal of Environmental Education).

With a Christian perspective, you can help kids understand that everything they do for God's creation they do for God. Every effort is a success story. And together, your kids can learn about what other groups are doing for God's creation, can undertake projects together, can support each other, can remind each other to keep the environmental focus on the Creator, and can celebrate their many successes.

LEADER TIP
for Down to Earth

Circulate among the groups to offer help as needed. If a group has trouble coming up with problems or solutions, these ideas may help them out:

Servanthood—People might pollute the water that everyone uses. Because God wants us to put others first, we could leave a lake or river in good shape for others when we go swimming.

Outreach—Some people may not know that water pollution is a problem. We could educate people about what we can all do to take care of God's water resources.

Thankfulness—Sometimes we don't take the time to appreciate God for what he has given us. We could take a friend for a walk around a lake just to praise God for his creation.

Stewardship—Clean water is a limited resource. We could make sure we conserve water that has gone through the treatment process to make certain there is enough for everyone.

and to pray specifically that they and other Christians can live out their principles as they handle the environment.

Say: **We've discussed our appreciation for God's creation. We've discussed how <u>God wants us to care for the earth.</u> We've discussed how our Christian principles can direct our responses to God's creation. Now let's see how our actions can make a difference.**

POSITIVE REINFORCEMENT ▼

Reduce, Renew, Rejoice (10 to 15 minutes)

Say: **One acre of tropical forest is being destroyed every second. Between 1990 and 1995, sewage, poisons, and other pollutants caused eight thousand beach closures or advisories. In 1993, Americans threw away 14 billion pounds of packaging** ("Natural Resources Defense Council 25 Year Report"). Ask:

● **Do you think these statistics are accurate?**

● **Do you think citing statistics such as these motivates people to action or overwhelms them to apathy? Explain.**

● **How do statistics such as these affect your motivation? Explain.**

"People should think of us as **servants of Christ,** the ones **God has trusted** with his secrets. Now in this way those who are trusted with something valuable must show they are **worthy of that trust."**

—**1** Corinthians **4:1-2**

● **Do you do everything you can to protect God's creation? Why or why not?**

● **Can you do anything about problems like those cited in the statistics I read? If so, how?**

Say: **Environmental problems often seem too large. We give up trying to solve problems because we can't ever do enough. Our contributions seem too insignificant. Let's have a relay race to see whether our efforts really add up to anything.**

Have kids form teams of four, then have teams line up at one end of the room. At the opposite end, in one corner, separate the aluminum cans into piles of ten. Be sure to provide one pile for each team. Place the cardboard box nearby. On the wall of the other corner, post the statistic that you prepared before the study. Place a marker on the floor by the newsprint.

Say: **To complete this relay, the first member of your team will run to the recycling box, stomp on an aluminum can, and put the can into the recycling box. Then that person will run to the newsprint, write "1," and run back to his or her team. Then that person will link elbows with the next person in his or her team's line and will repeat the process, each stomping on a can and each writing "1" on the newsprint** (see diagram p. 54). **Continue this until everyone on your team is linked together.**

Answer any question students have, then start the relay.

When everyone has finished the relay, gather kids together in front of the newsprint, and say: **Sometimes we feel as if nothing we do makes a real impact. That can lead to frustration or apathy. But let's see what a difference we really made when we worked together.** Revise the statistic on the newsprint to fit your group's efforts. First count the number of 1s the kids wrote, and fill that number in over the "one" in the statistic. Then multiply that number by eight, and fill in the new number in place of "eight" gallons of gasoline. For example, if you count twenty 1s, you'd write, "Recycling twenty aluminum cans saves the energy equivalent of about 160 gallons of gasoline." Ask:

● **What does the original statistic say about how individuals make a difference?**

● **What does the revised statistic say about how working together makes a difference?**

● **Did this relay change the way you'll look at your contribution? If so, how? If not, why not?**

Say: **Environmental problems can seem overwhelming, but both as individuals and in groups, we can make an incredible difference. After all, every effort we make is an effort to do God's will. Because <u>God wants you to care for the earth,</u> you praise and obey God every time you make an effort.** *That's* **daily success!**

LEADER TIP
for Reduce, Renew, Rejoice

If you decide to use one can per person, have every person stomp on one can only. Continue to have kids link arms to do the relay, but have just one person recycle a can and write a "1" during each round.

LEADER TIP
for Reduce, Renew, Rejoice

If your group isn't divisible by four, make some teams of five. In each team of five, have the first two people link arms and run the relay together, alternating responsibilities throughout the race.

Reduce, Renew, Rejoice Relay

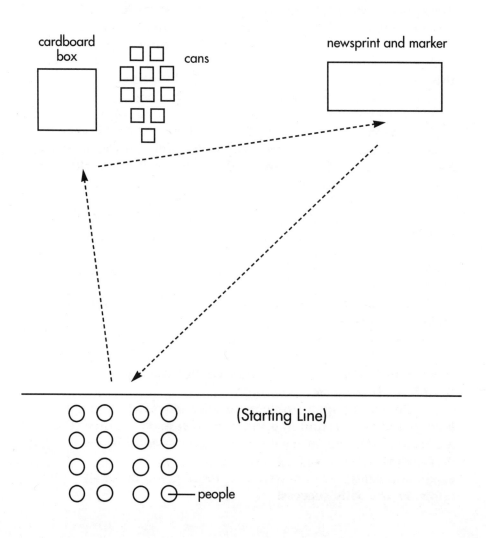

cardboard box

cans

newsprint and marker

(Starting Line)

people

Green
W A R S

Some say...

The environment is just fine. After all, people are living longer and healthier lives than ever before. Even scientists don't agree. Some say we're about to enter another ice age, and others say we're about to burn up from a lack of ozone-layer protection.

The state of the environment doesn't have anything to do with Christianity or the church. People who confuse the two are guilty of pantheism (everything in the universe is God) and idolatry—they're worshiping the things of nature instead of the Creator. The Bible gives clear directives, and it speaks pointedly against worshiping anything or anyone but God.

God created humans last. He gave us minds like those of no other creatures, and so he gave us dominion *over* nature. He not only gave us control of the earth, but he also told us to use it.

Environmentalists are missing the boat. Jesus told us to love our neighbors as ourselves. Instead, they put the welfare of animals, plants, and even bugs over the welfare of other people.

And some say...

The environment is in big trouble. More and more people are getting illnesses—such as certain cancers, lead poisoning, and diseases from polluted water—that are directly related to environmental problems. And even if scientists differ slightly in their prognoses, most do agree that many parts of the environment, from water to air to land, are unhealthy.

The environment brings people closer to God—who but God could have created something as beautiful and complex as the earth, its systems, and all its inhabitants? Praising God and appreciating his creation is completely different from worshiping nature itself. The Bible gives clear directives, and it speaks pointedly about acknowledging and praising God for his goodness.

God created humans last as caretakers of his creation. He gave humans minds like those of no other creatures, and so he gave us the responsibility to *care* for the earth—not dominate it or use it unwisely.

If you're not an environmentalist, you're missing the boat. Jesus told us to love our neighbors as ourselves. When you fight for God's creation—including animals, plants, and bugs—you contribute to everyone's well-being.

why ▼Active and Interactive Learning works with teenagers

Let's Start With the Big Picture

Think back to a major life lesson you've learned.
Got it? Now answer these questions:
● Did you learn your lesson from something you read?
● Did you learn it from something you heard?
● Did you learn it from something you experienced?
If you're like 99 percent of your peers, you answered "yes" only to the third question—you learned your life lesson from something you experienced.

This simple test illustrates the most convincing reason for using active and interactive learning with young people: People learn best through experience. Or to put it even more simply, people learn by doing.

Learning by doing is what active learning is all about. No more sitting quietly in chairs and listening to a speaker expound theories about God—that's passive learning. Active learning gets kids out of their chairs and into the experience of life. With active learning, kids get to *do* what they're studying. They *feel* the effects of the principles you teach. They *learn* by experiencing truth firsthand.

Active learning works because it recognizes three basic learning needs and uses them in concert to enable young people to make discoveries on their own and to find practical life applications for the truths they believe.

So what are these three basic learning needs?
1. Teenagers need action.
2. Teenagers need to think.
3. Teenagers need to talk.
Read on to find out exactly how these needs will be met by using the active and interactive learning techniques in Group's Core Belief Bible Study Series in your youth group.

1. Teenagers Need Action

Aircraft pilots know well the difference between passive and active learning. Their passive learning comes through listening to flight instructors and reading flight-instruction books. Their active learning comes through actually flying an airplane or flight simulator. Books and lectures may be helpful, but pilots really learn to fly by manipulating a plane's controls themselves.

We can help young people learn in a similar way. Though we may engage students passively in some reading and listening to teachers, their understanding and application of God's Word will really take off through simulated and real-life experiences.

Forms of active learning include simulation games; role-plays; service projects; experiments; research projects; group pantomimes; mock trials; construction projects; purposeful games; field trips; and, of course, the most powerful form of active learning—real-life experiences.

We can more fully explain active learning by exploring four of its characteristics:

● **Active learning is an adventure.** Passive learning is almost always predictable. Students sit passively while the teacher or speaker follows a planned outline or script.

In active learning, kids may learn lessons the teacher never envisioned. Because the leader trusts students to help create the learning experience, learners may venture into unforeseen discoveries. And often the teacher learns as much as the students.

● **Active learning is fun and captivating.** What are we communicating when we say, "OK, the fun's over—time to talk about God"? What's the hidden message? That joy is separate from God? And that learning is separate from joy?

What a shame.

Active learning is not joyless. One seventh-grader we interviewed clearly remembered her best Sunday school lesson: "Jesus was the light, and we went into a dark room and shut off the lights. We had a candle, and we learned that Jesus is the light and the dark can't shut off the light." That's active learning. Deena enjoyed the lesson. She had fun. And she learned.

Active learning intrigues people. Whether they find a foot-washing experience captivating or maybe a bit uncomfortable, they learn. And they learn on a level deeper than any work sheet or teacher's lecture could ever reach.

● **Active learning involves everyone.** Here the difference between passive and active learning becomes abundantly clear. It's like the difference between watching a football game on television and actually playing in the game.

The "trust walk" provides a good example of involving everyone in active learning. Half of the group members put on blindfolds; the other half serve as guides. The "blind" people trust the guides to lead them through the building or outdoors. The guides prevent the blind people from falling down stairs or tripping over rocks. Everyone needs to participate to learn the inherent lessons of trust, faith, doubt, fear, confidence, and servanthood. Passive spectators of this experience would learn little, but participants learn a great deal.

● **Active learning is focused through debriefing.** Activity simply for activity's sake doesn't usually result in good learning. Debriefing—evaluating an experience by discussing it in pairs or small groups—helps focus the experience and draw out its meaning. Debriefing helps sort and order the information students gather during the experience. It helps learners relate the recently experienced activity to their lives.

The process of debriefing is best started immediately after an experience. We use a three-step process in debriefing: reflection, interpretation, and application.

Reflection—This first step asks the students, "How did you feel?" Active-learning experiences typically evoke an emotional reaction, so it's appropriate to begin debriefing at that level.

Some people ask, "What do feelings have to do with education?" Feelings have everything to do with education. Think back again to that time in your life when you learned a big lesson. In all likelihood, strong feelings accompanied that lesson. Our emotions tend to cement things into our memories.

When you're debriefing, use open-ended questions to probe feelings. Avoid questions that can be answered with a "yes" or "no." Let your learners know that there are no wrong answers to these "feeling" questions. Everyone's feelings are valid.

Interpretation—The next step in the debriefing process asks, "What does this mean to you? How is this experience like or unlike some other aspect of your life?" Now you're asking people to identify a message or principle from the experience.

You want your learners to discover the message for themselves. So instead of telling students your answers, take the time to ask questions that encourage self-discovery. Use Scripture and discussion in pairs or small groups to explore how the actions and effects of the activity might translate to their lives.

Alert! Some of your people may interpret wonderful messages that you never intended. That's not failure! That's the Holy Spirit at work. God allows us to catch different glimpses of his kingdom even when we all look through the same glass.

Application—The final debriefing step asks, "What will you do about it?" This step moves learning into action. Your young people have shared a common experience. They've discovered a principle. Now they must create something new with what they've just experienced and interpreted. They must integrate the message into their lives.

The application stage of debriefing calls for a decision. Ask your students how they'll change, how they'll grow, what they'll do as a result of your time together.

2. Teenagers Need to Think

Today's students have been trained not to think. They aren't dumber than previous generations. We've simply conditioned them not to use their heads.

You see, we've trained our kids to respond with the simplistic answers they think the teacher wants to hear. Fill-in-the-blank student workbooks and teachers who ask dead-end questions such as "What's the capital of Delaware?" have produced kids and adults who have learned not to think.

And it doesn't just happen in junior high or high school. Our children are schooled very early not to think. Teachers attempt to help kids read with nonsensical fill-in-the-blank drills, word scrambles, and missing-letter puzzles.

Helping teenagers think requires a paradigm shift in how we teach. We need to plan for and set aside time for higher-order thinking and be willing to reduce our time spent on lower-order parroting. Group's Core Belief Bible Study Series is designed to help you do just that.

Thinking classrooms look quite different from traditional classrooms. In most church environments, the teacher does most of the talking and hopes that knowledge will transmit from his or her brain to the students'. In thinking settings, the teacher coaches students to ponder, wonder, imagine, and problem-solve.

3. Teenagers Need to Talk

Everyone knows that the person who learns the most in any class is the teacher. Explaining a concept to someone else is usually more helpful to the explainer than to the listener. So why not let the students do more teaching? That's one of the chief benefits of letting kids do the talking. This process is called interactive learning.

What is interactive learning? Interactive learning occurs when students discuss and work cooperatively in pairs or small groups.

Interactive learning encourages learners to work together. It honors the fact that students can learn from one another, not just from the teacher. Students work together in pairs or small groups to accomplish shared goals. They build together, discuss together, and present together. They teach each other and learn from one another. Success as a group is celebrated. Positive interdependence promotes individual and group learning.

Interactive learning not only helps people learn but also helps learners feel better about themselves and get along better with others. It accomplishes these things more effectively than the independent or competitive methods.

Here's a selection of interactive learning techniques that are used in Group's Core Belief Bible Study Series. With any of these models, leaders may assign students to specific partners or small groups. This will maximize cooperation and learning by preventing all the "rowdies" from linking up. And it will allow for new friendships to form outside of established cliques.

Following any period of partner or small-group work, the leader may reconvene the entire class for large-group processing. During this time the teacher may ask for reports or discoveries from individuals or teams. This technique builds in accountability for the teacherless pairs and small groups.

Pair-Share—With this technique each student turns to a partner and responds to a question or problem from the teacher or leader. Every learner responds. There are no passive observers. The teacher may then ask people to share their partners' responses.

Study Partners—Most curricula and most teachers call for Scripture passages to be read to the whole class by one person. One reads; the others doze.

Why not relinquish some teacher control and let partners read and react with each other? They'll all be involved—and will learn more.

Learning Groups—Students work together in small groups to create a model, design artwork, or study a passage or story; then they discuss what they learned through the experience. Each person in the learning group may be assigned a specific role. Here are some examples:

Reader

Recorder (makes notes of key thoughts expressed during the reading or discussion)

Checker (makes sure everyone understands and agrees with answers arrived at by the group)

Encourager (urges silent members to share their thoughts)

When everyone has a specific responsibility, knows what it is, and contributes to a small group, much is accomplished and much is learned.

Summary Partners—One student reads a paragraph, then the partner summarizes the paragraph or interprets its meaning. Partners alternate roles with each paragraph.

The paraphrasing technique also works well in discussions. Anyone who wishes to share a thought must first paraphrase what the previous person said. This sharpens listening skills and demonstrates the power of feedback communication.

Jigsaw—Each person in a small group examines a different concept, Scripture, or part of an issue. Then each teaches the others in the group. Thus, all members teach, and all must learn the others' discoveries. This technique is called a jigsaw because individuals are responsible to their group for different pieces of the puzzle.

JIGSAW EXAMPLE

Here's an example of a jigsaw.

Assign four-person teams. Have teammates each number off from one to four. Have all the Ones go to one corner of the room, all the Twos to another corner, and so on.

Tell team members they're responsible for learning information in their numbered corners and then for teaching their team members when they return to their original teams.

Give the following assignments to various groups:

Ones: Read Psalm 22. Discuss and list the prophecies made about Jesus.

Twos: Read Isaiah 52:13–53:12. Discuss and list the prophecies made

about Jesus.

Threes: Read Matthew 27:1-32. Discuss and list the things that happened to Jesus.

Fours: Read Matthew 27:33-66. Discuss and list the things that happened to Jesus.

After the corner groups meet and discuss, instruct all learners to return to their original teams and report what they've learned. Then have each team determine which prophecies about Jesus were fulfilled in the passages from Matthew.

Call on various individuals in each team to report one or two prophecies that were fulfilled.

You Can Do It Too!

All this information may sound revolutionary to you, but it's really not. God has been using active and interactive learning to teach his people for generations. Just look at Abraham and Isaac, Jacob and Esau, Moses and the Israelites, Ruth and Boaz. And then there's Jesus, who used active learning all the time!

Group's Core Belief Bible Study Series makes it easy for you to use active and interactive learning with your group. The active and interactive elements are automatically built in! Just follow the outlines, and watch as your kids grow through experience and positive interaction with others.

FOR DEEPER STUDY

For more information on incorporating active and interactive learning into your work with teenagers, check out these resources:

● *Why Nobody Learns Much of Anything at Church: And How to Fix It,* by Thom and Joani Schultz (Group Publishing) and

● *Do It! Active Learning in Youth Ministry,* by Thom and Joani Schultz (Group Publishing).

your evaluation of

Bible Study Series
for senior high

why CREATION matters

Group Publishing, Inc.
Attention: Core Belief Talk-Back
P.O. Box 481
Loveland, CO 80539
Fax: (970) 669-1994

Please help us continue to provide innovative and useful resources for ministry. After you've led the studies in this volume, take a moment to fill out this evaluation; then mail or fax it to us at the address above. Thanks!

● ● ● ● ● ●

1. As a whole, this book has been (circle one)

not very helpful   very helpful
1   2   3   4   5   6   7   8   9   10

2. The best things about this book:

3. How this book could be improved:

4. What I will change because of this book:

5. Would you be interested in field-testing future Core Belief Bible Studies and giving us your feedback? If so, please complete the information below:

Name _____

Street address _____

City _____ State _____ Zip _____

Daytime telephone (____) _____ Date _____

THANKS!